THE A TO Z OF EMOTIONAL REGULATION FOR CHILDREN

THERAPY-BASED STRATEGIES TO HELP LITTLE KIDS MANAGE BIG EMOTIONS CONFIDENTLY AND CALMLY

Copyright © 2024 by Máire Powell

All rights reserved.

No part of this book may be reproduced in any form or by any electronic or mechanical means, including information storage and retrieval systems, without written permission from the author, except for the use of brief quotations in a book review.

For the little ones with big feelings—neurodiverse minds, brave hearts, and all those figuring out life's emotional rollercoaster. You've got this, and this book's got you!

DEAR PARENTS, EDUCATORS, AND THERAPISTS,

Thank you for choosing this book as a tool to support the children in your care. You're about to embark on a meaningful journey into the world of emotional regulation—a skill that is essential for navigating life's challenges with confidence and calm.

Emotional regulation is like a superpower—it allows children to manage their feelings, stay grounded in difficult moments, and approach life with resilience. From anger to joy, every emotion has its place, and this book provides practical tools to help children to process, and regulate these feelings in ways that are both accessible and effective.

Each activity, tip, and technique in this book is carefully backed by evidence-based theories and therapeutic interventions, such as Cognitive Behavioral Therapy, Emotion-Focused Therapy and others.

This book is structured around the alpha-bet, introducing a different emotion or idea with each letter. From "A for Anger" to "Z for Zen," you'll find clear, simple exercises and tools that empower children to build emotional resilience. As you use this book, remember that emotional regulation is a skill built over time—through practice, patience, and encouragement. Together, let's help children discover their emotional superpowers, creating a foundation of strength and self-awareness that will serve them throughout their lives.

Warm regards,
Máire

A - Anger

Anger is like a storm inside you—big, loud, and sometimes hard to control. But did you know you can calm the storm?

⭐ **Try This**: Slowly count to ten when you feel anger bubbling up. Or, take a break in a "calm corner," a cozy spot where you can relax and breathe.

Theory/Therapy: CBT

Strategy: Helps children identify and challenge negative thoughts while providing practical techniques like counting to ten to regulate emotions.

B - Breathe Deeply

Breathing isn't just something you do all the time—it's also a way to help you feel calm and strong.

⭐ **Try This:** Practice "box breathing." Breathe in for four counts, hold your breath for four counts, breathe out for four counts, and hold again for four counts. Imagine drawing a square as you breathe.

Theory/Therapy: Mindfulness-Based Stress Reduction

Strategy: Deep breathing exercises are central to mindfulness, reducing stress and promoting calm.

C - Calm

Chaos happens, but you can find your calm anytime with your imagination.

⭐ **Try This:** Close your eyes and picture a peaceful place, like a sunny beach or a cozy forest. Imagine yourself there, feeling safe and relaxed.

Theory/Therapy: Visualization Therapy

Strategy: Visualization techniques are often used to create a sense of calm and focus on positive mental imagery.

D - Disappointment

Feeling let down when things don't go as planned is okay. But guess what? There's always something good to find.

⭐ **Try This:** Write three things you're grateful for in a "Gratitude Journal." It's a great way to remember the happy moments.

Theory/Therapy: Positive Psychology

Strategy: Focusing on gratitude and reframing negative experiences to highlight positive aspects.

E - Excitement

Excitement can feel like fireworks inside you. Let's channel that energy into something amazing!

⭐ **Try This:** Use your excitement to create something fun, like a drawing, a song, or a cool dance move.

Theory/Therapy:
Behavioral Activation

Strategy: Encourages Challenging energy into productive and enjoyable activities.

F - Frustration

Feeling stuck is frustrating, but every problem has a solution.

⭐ **Try This:** When you feel frustrated, take a deep breath and break the task into smaller steps. Celebrate each step you complete!

Theory/Therapy: Problem-Solving
Strategy: Guides children in breaking down challenges into smaller, manageable steps.

G - Gratitude

Gratitude is like magic—it turns small moments into big smiles.

⭐ **Try This:** At the end of each day, think of three good things that happened, no matter how small. Write them down or share them with someone you love.

Theory/Therapy: Positive Psychology

Strategy: Practicing gratitude boosts happiness and emotional well-being.

H - Happiness

Happiness is everywhere—it's in the little moments and big laughs.

⭐ **Try This:** Smile and think about a happy memory. Sharing it with a friend makes it even better.

Theory/Therapy: Joyful Play Therapy

Strategy: Engage children in activities that naturally foster happiness and social connection.

I - Identify Your Feelings

Understanding what you're feeling is the first step to managing it. Every emotion has a name, and giving it one can help you feel more in control.

> ⭐ **Try This:** Pause and ask yourself, "What am I feeling right now?" Use a feelings chart or list to find the word that matches your emotion. You might say, "I feel angry," or "I feel excited." Once you name it, you can take the next step to handle it.

Theory/Therapy: Emotion-Focused Therapy (EFT)

Strategy: Naming emotions increases awareness and helps reduce emotional distress. Recognizing feelings like anger or excitement provides a foundation for taking constructive action.

J - Jealousy

It's okay to feel jealous sometimes. Use it as inspiration!

⭐**Try This:** Consider how to turn jealousy into motivation to reach your goals. Clap for others' success—it's a powerful habit.

Theory/Therapy: Social Learning Theory
Strategy: Encourages observing and modeling positive behaviors, such as celebrating others' achievements.

K - Kindness

Kindness is a gift you give to yourself and others.

⭐**Try This:** Do one kind thing for someone today, like sharing a toy or saying something nice. It feels incredible to make someone smile.

Theory/Therapy: Compassion-Focused Therapy
Strategy: Cultivates kindness toward others fostering social connection and reducing stress.

L - Loneliness

Feeling lonely doesn't mean you're alone. Someone always cares about you.

⭐ **Try This:** Call a friend or family member and talk about your day. Connecting with someone can brighten your mood.

Theory/Therapy: Attachment Theory
Strategy: Encourages reaching out to trusted individuals, reinforcing the importance of secure relationships.

M - Mindfulness

Mindfulness helps you stay in the present moment and enjoy it fully.

⭐ **Try This:** Practice the "Five Senses Exercise." Sit quietly and notice: Five things you can see. Four things you can touch. Three things you can hear. Two things you can smell. One thing you can taste.

Theory/Therapy: Mindfulness-Based Cognitive Therapy

Strategy: Teaches mindfulness practices to enhance emotional regulation.

N - Nervousness

It's normal to feel nervous about new experiences. You can turn those jitters into confidence.

⭐**Try This:** Practice self-talk. Say, "I've got this," or, "I'm brave." Plan ahead to feel more prepared.

Theory/Therapy: Cognitive-Behavioral Therapy

Strategy: Uses self-talk and planning to reduce anxiety and increase confidence.

O - Optimism

Looking on the bright side can make challenges feel smaller and life feel lighter.

⭐ **Try This:** Ask yourself, "What if everything goes right?" Imagine the best possible outcome and focus on it.

Theory/Therapy: Positive Psychology

Strategy: Encourages focusing on positive outcomes and building resilence.

P - Perseverance

Sometimes tasks feel challenging, but sticking with them makes you stronger.

⭐**Try This:** Break big tasks into small steps. Celebrate each success, no matter how small.

Theory/Therapy: Growth Mindset Theory

Strategy: Reinforces the belief that effort and persistence lead to success.

Q - Quiet Time

Everyone needs time to rest and recharge, even superheroes.

⭐ **Try This:** Create a quiet space just for you. Fill it with things you love, like books, blankets, or soft lights.

Theory/Therapy: Self-care and Relaxation tectniques

Strategy: Promotes taking breaks to recharge and maintain emotional balance.

R - Restlessness

Feeling wiggly? That's your body's way of saying it needs to move!

⭐**Try This:** Do a quick stretch, some jumping jacks, or even a silly dance to release extra energy.

Theory/Therapy: Physical Activity and Emotional Regulation

Strategy: Uses movement to release pent-up energy and refocus attention.

S - Self-Control

Learning to pause before you react is a superpowers

⭐**Try This:** Use the "stoplight method." When you feel upset, imagine a stoplight:
- Red: Stop and take a breath.
- Yellow: Think about your choices.
- Green: Go with the best one.

Theory/Therapy: Emotional Regulation Strategies

Strategy: The "stoplight method" integrates stopping, thinking, and acting as a framework for controlling impulses.

T - Tears and Sadness

It's okay to cry. Tears are how your heart lets go of sadness.

⭐**Try This:** Hug a favorite stuffed animal, pet, or family member. Hugs can help you feel better.

Theory/Therapy: Acceptance and Commitment Therapy ACT

Strategy: Encourages acceptance of emotions and using comforting activities to process sadness.

U - Understanding Others

Empathy means putting yourself in someone esle's shoes.

⭐ **Try This:** Play a "superhero" game where you imagine how you can help someone who's feeling upset.

Theory/Therapy: Empathy Training and Social Skills.

Strategy: Enhances perspective-taking and fosters interpersonal understanding.

V - Victory

Every time you achieve something, no matter how small, it's a victory worth celebrating.

⭐**Try This:** Reward yourself for a job well done, even if it's just giving yourself a high-five or saying, "Great job, me!"

Theory/Therapy: Positive Reinforcement (Operant Conditioning)

Strategy: Celebrating small wins builds confidence and reinforces persistence.

W - Worry

Worries can feel heavy, but you don't have to carry them around.

⭐ **Try This:** Write down your worries on paper and crumple them up. Toss them in the trash and imagine them disappearing.

Theory/Therapy: Cognitive-Behavioral Therapy

Strategy: Techniques like writing worries down externalize and reduce anxiety.

X - eXercise

Moving your body can help your mind feel better too!

⭐**Try This:** Dance to your favorite song, stretch, jump or run in place. Any movement works!

Theory/Therapy: Physical Exercise and Emotional Regulation

Strategy: Engages the body to improve mood and manage stress.

Y - You Are Enough

You're amazing, just as you are!

⭐ **Try This:** Look in the mirror and say, "I am awesome. I can do great things." Repeat it often!

Theory/Therapy: Self-Compassion Theory

Strategy: Builds self-esteem and encourages self-acceptance through affirmations.

Z - Zen Moments

Zen is about finding peace, even when things are noisy or busy.

⭐ **Try This:** Sit cross-legged, close your eyes, and take deep breaths. Imagine your favorite calming sounds, like waves or soft music.

Theory/Therapy: Meditation and Relaxation Techniques

Strategy: Practices like meditation create moments of peace and emotional clarity.

CONCLUSION

Wow, look at you go! You've just finished exploring the A to Z of emotional regulation—a toolkit full of awesome strategies to help you understand and manage your feelings. That's such a big step, and you should be proud of yourself!

But here's the secret: learning these skills doesn't stop here. The more you practice these techniques, the stronger and more confident you'll become. Try using one or two ideas every day, and don't worry if it feels tricky at first—it takes time to build new habits. And guess what? You have someone right here to help you along the way.

Ask your grown-up—whether it's your parent, teacher, or therapist—to read this book with you again whenever you want.

Together, you can explore different strategies, practice them in new ways, and talk about what works best for you. Emotions are like puzzles; sometimes you need to try different pieces to see what fits.

Every time you open this book, you'll find new ways to feel calm, strong, and in control of your emotions. Some days you might need "A for Anger," and other days "Z for Zen" will be just what you're looking for. And that's the best part—this book will always be here to guide you when you need it.

So, keep practicing, keep trying, and keep learning. You're growing stronger every single day, and you're not alone. Your grown-up is right here to help you, cheer you on, and remind you: You've got this!

Now go and use your emotional superpowers you're amazing!

Thank you for reading The A-to-Z of Emotional Regulation for Kids! If you found this book helpful, please consider leaving a review on Amazon or recommending it to others—your feedback makes a difference and helps more families discover this resource.

www.ingramcontent.com/pod-product-compliance
Lightning Source LLC
Chambersburg PA
CBHW082214070526
44585CB00020B/2416

6. Powell, M. (2023). *Executive Functioning Superpowers: Inclusive Strategies That Embrace Neurodiversity at Home and in the Classroom.* Available at Amazon.
Provides practical strategies for improving executive functioning and emotional regulation in children, with a focus on embracing neurodiversity.

7. Seligman, M. E. P. (2011). *Flourish: A Visionary New Understanding of Happiness and Well-Being.* Atria Books. A guide to building well-being through positive psychology principles.

8. Shapiro, L. E. (2004). *The Relaxation and Stress Reduction Workbook for Kids.* New Harbinger Publications.
Provides children with accessible tools for managing stress and emotions.

9. Siegel, D. J., & Bryson, T. P. (2011). *The Whole-Brain Child: 12 Revolutionary Strategies to Nurture Your Child's Developing Mind.* Bantam Books.
Offers strategies to help children integrate their emotional and logical minds for better regulation.

REFERENCES AND FURTHER READING FOR PARENTS, EDUCATORS AND THERAPISTS

Books and Research Supporting Emotional Regulation for Children:

1. Dweck, C. S. (2006). *Mindset: The New Psychology of Success*. Random House.
Explores how a growth mindset can help individuals develop resilience and perseverance.

2. Gottman, J. M., & DeClaire, J. (1997). *Raising an Emotionally Intelligent Child*. Simon & Schuster.
Offers strategies for helping children understand and regulate their emotions.

3. Kabat-Zinn, J. (1994). *Wherever You Go, There You Are: Mindfulness Meditation in Everyday Life*. Hachette Books.
Introduces mindfulness practices for reducing stress and improving focus.

4. Linehan, M. M. (2015). *DBT Skills Training Manual*. Guilford Press.
A practical guide to emotional regulation techniques from Dialectical Behavior Therapy.

5. Neff, K. (2011). *Self-Compassion: The Proven Power of Being Kind to Yourself*. HarperCollins.
Discusses how self-compassion can enhance emotional resilience and self-esteem.